Holiday Planner

This planner belongs to:

Name: ....

Phone: ....

Holiday Card List

Name
....

Sent?
☐

Address
....

....

....

Name
....

Sent?
☐

Address
....

....

....

Name
....

Sent?
☐

Address
....

....

....

Name
....

Sent?
☐

Address
....

....

....

Name
....

Sent?
☐

Address
....

....

....

Name
....

Sent?
☐

Address
....

....

....

Holiday Card List

Name .... Sent ?

Address .... ☐

....

....

Name .... Sent ?

Address .... ☐

....

....

Name .... Sent ?

Address .... ☐

....

....

Name .... Sent ?

Address .... ☐

....

....

Name .... Sent ?

Address .... ☐

....

....

Name .... Sent ?

Address .... ☐

....

....

Holiday Card List

Name   Sent?

Address   ☐

....

....

Name   Sent?

Address   ☐

....

....

Name   Sent?

Address   ☐

....

....

Name   Sent?

Address   ☐

....

....

Name   Sent?

Address   ☐

....

....

Name   Sent?

Address   ☐

....

....

Holiday Card List

Name .... Sent ?

Address .... ☐

....

....

Name .... Sent ?

Address .... ☐

....

....

Name .... Sent ?

Address .... ☐

....

....

Name .... Sent ?

Address .... ☐

....

....

Name .... Sent ?

Address .... ☐

....

....

Name .... Sent ?

Address .... ☐

....

....

Holiday Card List

Name

Address

Sent? ☐

Name

Address

Sent? ☐

Name

Address

Sent? ☐

Name

Address

Sent? ☐

Name

Address

Sent? ☐

Name

Address

Sent? ☐

Holiday Card List

Name .... Sent?

Address .... ☐

....

....

Name .... Sent?

Address .... ☐

....

....

Name .... Sent?

Address .... ☐

....

....

Name .... Sent?

Address .... ☐

....

....

Name .... Sent?

Address .... ☐

....

....

Name .... Sent?

Address .... ☐

....

....

Holiday Card List

Name

Address

Name

Address

Name

Address

Name

Address

Name

Address

Name

Address

Holiday Card List

Name   Sent ?

Address .... ☐

....

....

Name   Sent ?

Address .... ☐

....

....

Name   Sent ?

Address .... ☐

....

....

Name   Sent ?

Address .... ☐

....

....

Name   Sent ?

Address .... ☐

....

....

Name   Sent ?

Address .... ☐

....

....

Holiday Card List

Name

.... Sent?

Address

....

....

....

Name

.... Sent?

Address

....

....

....

Name

.... Sent?

Address

....

....

....

Name

.... Sent?

Address

....

....

....

Name

.... Sent?

Address

....

....

....

Name

.... Sent?

Address

....

....

....

Holiday Card List

Name   *Sent ?*

Address

....

....

Name   *Sent ?*

Address

....

....

Name   *Sent ?*

Address

....

....

Name   *Sent ?*

Address

....

....

Name   *Sent ?*

Address

....

....

Name   *Sent ?*

Address

....

....

Holiday Card List

Name   Sent?

Address ⬜

....

....

Name   Sent?

Address ⬜

....

....

Name   Sent?

Address ⬜

....

....

Name   Sent?

Address ⬜

....

....

Name   Sent?

Address ⬜

....

....

Name   Sent?

Address ⬜

....

....

Holiday Card List

Name   Sent ?

Address

Name   Sent ?

Address

Name   Sent ?

Address

Name   Sent ?

Address

Name   Sent ?

Address

Name   Sent ?

Address

Holiday Card List

Name
....   Sent?
Address
....   ☐

....

....

Name
....   Sent?
Address
....   ☐

....

....

Name
....   Sent?
Address
....   ☐

....

....

Name
....   Sent?
Address
....   ☐

....

....

Name
....   Sent?
Address
....   ☐

....

....

Name
....   Sent?
Address
....   ☐

....

....

Holiday Card List

Name
Sent ?

Address

Name
Sent ?

Address

Name
Sent ?

Address

Name
Sent ?

Address

Name
Sent ?

Address

Name
Sent ?

Address

# Holiday Card List

Name
.... Sent?
Address
....
....
....

Name
.... Sent?
Address
....
....
....

Name
.... Sent?
Address
....
....
....

Name
.... Sent?
Address
....
....
....

Name
.... Sent?
Address
....
....
....

Name
.... Sent?
Address
....
....
....

Holiday Card List

Name   Sent?

Address

....

....

Name   Sent?

Address

....

....

Name   Sent?

Address

....

....

Name   Sent?

Address

....

....

Name   Sent?

Address

....

....

Name   Sent?

Address

....

....

Holiday Card List

Name	Sent ?
Address	☐
....	
....	
Name	Sent ?
Address	☐
....	
....	
Name	Sent ?
Address	☐
....	
....	
Name	Sent ?
Address	☐
....	
....	
Name	Sent ?
Address	☐
....	
....	
Name	Sent ?
Address	☐
....	
....	

Holiday Card List

Name .... Sent ?

Address ....

....

....

Name .... Sent ?

Address ....

....

....

Name .... Sent ?

Address ....

....

....

Name .... Sent ?

Address ....

....

....

Name .... Sent ?

Address ....

....

....

Name .... Sent ?

Address ....

....

....

Holiday Card List

Name
....

Address
....

....

....

Sent?
☐

Name
....

Address
....

....

....

Sent?
☐

Name
....

Address
....

....

....

Sent?
☐

Name
....

Address
....

....

....

Sent?
☐

Name
....

Address
....

....

....

Sent?
☐

Name
....

Address
....

....

....

Sent?
☐

Holiday Card List

Name

Sent?

Address

....

....

Name

Sent?

Address

....

....

Name

Sent?

Address

....

....

Name

Sent?

Address

....

....

Name

Sent?

Address

....

....

Name

Sent?

Address

....

....

Holiday Card List

Name
....

Address
....

....

....

Name
....

Address
....

....

....

Name
....

Address
....

....

....

Name
....

Address
....

....

....

Name
....

Address
....

....

....

Name
....

Address
....

....

....

Sent?

Sent?

Sent?

Sent?

Sent?

Sent?

Holiday Card List

Name

Sent?

Address

Name

Sent?

Address

Name

Sent?

Address

Name

Sent?

Address

Name

Sent?

Address

Name

Sent?

Address

Holiday Card List

Name

....

Address

....

....

....

Sent?

☐

Name

....

Address

....

....

....

Sent?

☐

Name

....

Address

....

....

....

Sent?

☐

Name

....

Address

....

....

....

Sent?

☐

Name

....

Address

....

....

....

Sent?

☐

Name

....

Address

....

....

....

Sent?

☐

Holiday Card List

Name   Sent?
....
Address
....

....

....

Name   Sent?
....
Address
....

....

....

Name   Sent?
....
Address
....

....

....

Name   Sent?
....
Address
....

....

....

Name   Sent?
....
Address
....

....

....

Name   Sent?
....
Address
....

....

....

Holiday Card List

Name

        Sent ?

Address

....

....

Name

        Sent ?

Address

....

....

Name

        Sent ?

Address

....

....

Name

        Sent ?

Address

....

....

Name

        Sent ?

Address

....

....

Name

        Sent ?

Address

....

....

Holiday Card List

Name .... Sent ?

Address ....

....

....

Name .... Sent ?

Address ....

....

....

Name .... Sent ?

Address ....

....

....

Name .... Sent ?

Address ....

....

....

Name .... Sent ?

Address ....

....

....

Name .... Sent ?

Address ....

....

....

Holiday Card List

Name
....

Address
....

....

....

Sent?
☐

Name
....

Address
....

....

....

Sent?
☐

Name
....

Address
....

....

....

Sent?
☐

Name
....

Address
....

....

....

Sent?
☐

Name
....

Address
....

....

....

Sent?
☐

Name
....

Address
....

....

....

Sent?
☐

Holiday Card List

Name ....
Sent ?
Address ....
☐
....
....

Name ....
Sent ?
Address ....
☐
....
....

Name ....
Sent ?
Address ....
☐
....
....

Name ....
Sent ?
Address ....
☐
....
....

Name ....
Sent ?
Address ....
☐
....
....

Name ....
Sent ?
Address ....
☐
....
....

Gift List/Ideas

Immediate Family

Name   Store/Website

....

....

....

....

....

....

....

Name   Store/Website

....

....

....

....

....

....

Name   Store/Website

....

....

....

....

....

....

Gift List/Ideas

Immediate Family

Name   Store/Website

···
···
···
···
···
···
···

Name   Store/Website

···
···
···
···
···
···
···

Name   Store/Website

···
···
···
···
···
···
···

Gift List/Ideas

Immediate Family

Name   **Store/Website**

....

....

....

....

....

....

....

Name   **Store/Website**

....

....

....

....

....

....

....

Name   **Store/Website**

....

....

....

....

....

....

....

Gift List/Ideas

Immediate Family

Name   Store/Website
....
....
....
....
....
....
....
....

Name   Store/Website
....
....
....
....
....
....
....
....

Name   Store/Website
....
....
....
....
....
....
....
....

Gift List/Ideas

Extended Family

Name Store/Website

....
....
....
....
....
....
....

Name Store/Website

....
....
....
....
....
....
....

Name Store/Website

....
....
....
....
....
....
....

Gift List/Ideas

Extended Family

Name   Store/Website

....

....

....

....

....

....

....

Name   Store/Website

....

....

....

....

....

....

....

Name   Store/Website

....

....

....

....

....

....

Gift List/Ideas

Friends/Neighbors

Name   Store/Website

....
....
....
....
....
....
....

Name   Store/Website

....
....
....
....
....
....
....

Name   Store/Website

....
....
....
....
....
....
....

Gift List/Ideas

Friends/Neighbors

Name   Store/Website
....
....
....
....
....
....
....

Name   Store/Website
....
....
....
....
....
....
....

Name   Store/Website
....
....
....
....
....
....
....

Gift List/Ideas

Co-workers, Boss, Teachers, Babysitters

Name   Store/Website
....
....
....
....
....
....
....
....

Name   Store/Website
....
....
....
....
....
....
....

Name   Store/Website
....
....
....
....
....
....
....

Gift List/Ideas

Mail Carrier, Delivery Driver, Hairdresser, etc

Name   Store/Website

....

....

....

....

....

....

....

Name   Store/Website

....

....

....

....

....

....

Name   Store/Website

....

....

....

....

....

....

Gingerbread Martinis

Ginger liqueur
Crushed gingersnaps
2 tablespoons ginger liqueur
2 tablespoons vanilla vodka
1 tablespoons coffee-flavored rum

1 tablespoon honey
2 teaspoons whipping cream
1 cup ice cubes
Garnish: cinnamon, candy cane

Preparation:

Dip glass rims in ginger liqueur and crushed gingersnaps. Store glasses in freezer up to 2 days.

Stir together 2 Tbsp. ginger liqueur, vanilla vodka, coffee-flavored rum, honey, and whipping cream in a cocktail shaker. Add ice cubes, cover with lid, and shake vigorously until well chilled. Strain into a chilled martini glass. Garnish, if desired.

Favorite Recipe

Name:

Ingredients:
....
....
....
....
....
....
....
....
....
....
....
....

Preparation:
....
....
....
....
....
....
....
....
....
....
....
....

RUDOLPH SPRITZERS

5 cups orange juice

1 cup cranberry juice

2 cups chilled lemon-lime soft drink

1 1/2 cups vodka

Garnishes: orange slices, fresh rosemary sprigs

Preparation:

1. Stir together all ingredients; serve over ice.
Garnish, if desired.

Favorite Recipe

Name:

Ingredients:

....
....
....
....
....
....
....
....
....
....
....
....

Preparation:

....
....
....
....
....
....
....
....
....
....
....
....
....

Artichoke Salsa

1 jar (6.5 ounces) marinated artichoke hearts, undrained
1 large red pepper
1/4 cup pitted ripe black olives, chopped
1/4 cup chopped red onion
1/2 teaspoon garlic paste
2 tablespoons fresh basil leaves, chopped
sea salt and ground pepper to taste

Preparation:
Drain artichokes, keeping marinade in bowl. Chop artichokes and red pepper. Add all ingredients to marinade and stir. Season to taste with salt and pepper. Serve with crispy bread or tortilla chips.

Favorite Recipe

Name:

Ingredients:

....
....
....
....
....
....
....
....
....
....
....
....

Preparation:

....
....
....
....
....
....
....
....
....
....
....
....
....

Vidalia Onion Dip

2 large vidalia onions
1 cup shredded swiss cheese
1 cup shredded parmesan cheese
3/4 cup mayonnaise
1 teaspoon worcestershire sauce

Preparation:

Chop onions. Combine all ingredients in large bowl. Spread all ingredients in greased, small baking dish. bake at 350 for 30 minutes or until lightly browned and bubbly. Serve with crackers.

Favorite Recipe

Name:

Ingredients:
....
....
....
....
....
....
....
....
....
....
....
....

Preparation:
....
....
....
....
....
....
....
....
....
....
....
....

FRUIT PIZZA

1 16.5 ounce refrigerated sugar cookie dough
1 8 ounce package cream cheese, softened
6 tablespoons sugar
4 kiwis
3 packages of fresh
strawberries, raspberries or mixed

Glaze:
1/2 cup orange juice
1/4 cup lemon juice
1/4 cup water
1/2 cup sugar
2 tablespoons cornstarch

Preparation:
Press softened dough into greased pizza pan or cookie sheet.
Bake at 375 for 15-20 minutes. Let cool in refrigerator. While
cooling, slice fruit. Mix cream cheese with 6 tablespoons sugar
and spread over cooled cookie. Arrange fruit on top of cream
cheese mixture. Put glaze ingredients in a saucepan and bring
to a low boil. Reduce heat and let simmer until thick and bubbly.
Let cool about 15 minutes and spread over fruit

Favorite Recipe

Name:

Ingredients:

....
....
....
....
....
....
....
....
....
....
....
....

Preparation:

....
....
....
....
....
....
....
....
....
....
....
....

Meal Planning

Shopping List

....
....
....
....

....
....
....
....

....
....
....
....

....
....
....
....

....
....
....
....

....
....
....
....

Meal Planning

....
....
....
....
....
....
....
....
....
....
....
....
....
....
....
....
....
....
....
....
....
....
....
....

Shopping List

....

....

....

....

....

....

....

....

....

....

....

....

....

....

....

....

....

....

....

....

....

....

....

....

Meal Planning

Shopping List

Meal Planning

....
....
....
....

....
....
....
....

....
....
....
....

....
....
....
....

....
....
....
....

....
....
....
....

Shopping List

....

....

....

....

....

....

....

....

....

....

....

....

....

....

....

....

....

....

....

....

....

....

Meal Planning

Shopping List

Holiday Memories

Holiday Memories

Holiday Memories

Holiday Memories

Holiday Happenings
{things to do together this season}

....

....

....

....

....

....

....

....

....

....

....

....

....

....

....

....

....

....

....

....

....

....

....

....

Holiday Happenings
{things to do together this season}

....
....
....
....

....
....
....
....

....
....
....
....

....
....
....
....

....
....
....
....

....
....
....
....

Thank You List

Name .... Sent?

Gift .... ☐

....

....

Name .... Sent?

Gift .... ☐

....

....

Name .... Sent?

Gift .... ☐

....

....

Name .... Sent?

Gift .... ☐

....

....

Name .... Sent?

Gift .... ☐

....

....

Name .... Sent?

Gift .... ☐

....

....

Thank You List

Name .... Sent ?

Gift ....

....

....

Name .... Sent ?

Gift ....

....

....

Name .... Sent ?

Gift ....

....

....

Name .... Sent ?

Gift ....

....

....

Name .... Sent ?

Gift ....

....

....

Name .... Sent ?

Gift ....

....

....

Thank You List

Name
....
Gift
....

....

....

Sent?
☐

Name
....
Gift
....

....

....

Sent?
☐

Name
....
Gift
....

....

....

Sent?
☐

Name
....
Gift
....

....

....

Sent?
☐

Name
....
Gift
....

....

....

Sent?
☐

Name
....
Gift
....

....

....

Sent?
☐

Thank You List

Name .... Sent?

Gift ....

....

....

Name .... Sent?

Gift ....

....

....

Name .... Sent?

Gift ....

....

....

Name .... Sent?

Gift ....

....

....

Name .... Sent?

Gift ....

....

....

Name .... Sent?

Gift ....

....

....

Thank You List

Name .... Sent?

Gift .... ☐

....

....

Name .... Sent?

Gift .... ☐

....

....

Name .... Sent?

Gift .... ☐

....

....

Name .... Sent?

Gift .... ☐

....

....

Name .... Sent?

Gift .... ☐

....

....

Name .... Sent?

Gift .... ☐

....

....

Thank You List

Name .... Sent ?

Gift .... ☐

....

....

Name .... Sent ?

Gift .... ☐

....

....

Name .... Sent ?

Gift .... ☐

....

....

Name .... Sent ?

Gift .... ☐

....

....

Name .... Sent ?

Gift .... ☐

....

....

Name .... Sent ?

Gift .... ☐

....

....

Notes

Notes

Notes

Notes

Notes

Notes

Notes

Notes

Notes

Notes

Notes

Notes

Notes

···

···

···

···

···

···

···

···

···

···

···

···

···

···

···

···

···

···

···

···

···

Notes

Notes

Notes

Notes

Notes

Notes

Notes

Notes

Notes

Notes

Notes

Notes

Notes

Notes

CPSIA information can be obtained at www.ICGtesting.com
Printed in the USA
LVOW01*0822041114

411945LV00001B/3/P